W9-AGC-334

Teacher Therapy

Teacher Therapy

written by
Karen Katafiasz

illustrated by
R.W. Alley

ONE
CARING
PLACE

Abbey Press

Text © 1997 by Karen Katafiasz
Illustrations © 1997 by St. Meinrad Archabbey
Published by One Caring Place
Abbey Press
St. Meinrad, Indiana 47577

All rights reserved.
No part of this book may be used or reproduced in any manner
without written permission of the publisher, except in the case of
brief quotations embodied in critical articles and reviews.

Library of Congress Catalog Number
97-60487

ISBN 0-87029-302-8

Printed in the United States of America

Foreword

There's a wry adage that maintains the three best things about teaching are June, July, and August. As every teacher knows, at times that line hardly seems like a joke.

Teaching—if you do it right—is tough. Every student is utterly unique, with different learning styles and strengths, interests, experiences, and motivations. And each student places demands on you that require you to respond with your entire being—body, mind, and spirit.

No wonder teaching is more a calling than a job, needing as much talent and skill as any art. And no wonder you sometimes feel so depleted, so tired.

Teacher Therapy can't take away the tough times. It won't decrease your class size or correct your papers, plan your lessons or perfect your students.

But it does offer sound and realistic advice—for taking care of yourself, for bringing out the best in those you teach, for recognizing and respecting the power you have to change lives.

With its inspiring words and lighthearted illustrations, this pocket-size pep talk will renew the enthusiasm that stirred in your heart when you first knew that you were meant to be a teacher.

1.

To spend your life doing
what matters is the greatest
of all achievements. Teaching
matters.

2.

Remember those teachers who influenced your life for the good. What did they do? How did they give you what you needed? Follow their example.

3.

Be aware that you teach so much more than a subject. You are opening minds and hearts; you are shaping lives.

4.

Radiate enthusiasm for your students, for learning, for life—and for engaging students in learning and in life. Your students—and you—will be so much richer.

5.

Be passionate about the subject matter that you teach. Excitement is contagious.

6.

Listen to and respect your students' dreams. Then challenge them to reach even higher.

7.

Children need healthy structure and guidelines to learn and to grow well. Give your students rules that are firm, fair, and consistent.

8.

Act with honesty, justice, and integrity. By doing so, you teach these values without effort.

9.

Use good organization to increase your effectiveness and give your day structure. If you take work home, make a conscious decision to do so. You need time off to stay fresh and avoid burnout.

10.

When you ask your students to be responsible, you must be responsible to them. Honor your commitments; keep your promises.

11.

Teaching is demanding—take care of yourself physically. Have a healthy lunch, make time for exercise, get enough rest.

12.

Take care of yourself spiritually. Center yourself in God; be aware of God's presence in your classroom.

13.

Students need a classroom where they feel welcomed, safe, respected, challenged. Make your classroom that place.

14.

You have a great deal of power in the classroom—power to set the tone, power to make a child's time there miserable or joyful. Use your power for good.

15.

Teach your students that it's all right to make mistakes. Mistakes aren't reasons for shame but chances to learn and do better.

16.

There will be times when you won't easily relate to a student. Be aware of your feelings and preferences, and try to transcend them by striving to give every child equal attention and equal treatment.

17.

Offer basic acceptance to your students—not necessarily of their behavior but always of their being, their very existence. Even when you don't like your students, you can love them.

18.

There can be so much tugging at your students' minds and hearts—troubled family situations, changing friendships, uncertainties, doubts, and fears. Be aware of them as whole persons.

19.

Realize that for some students, school is a respite, a place of safety. Keep it a safe place for them to reveal themselves and to be themselves.

20.

Each day, you have the opportunity to offer your students the world, to give them life-changing knowledge and experiences. Relish the possibilities.

21.

Help your students to discover their strengths, to achieve, to excel. Satisfaction at what they accomplish will give them self-esteem.

22.

School can be the place where your students learn they're worthwhile and where they can counter unhealthy lessons they're learning elsewhere. Give them that chance.

23.

Take care of yourself mentally. Keep learning; follow your own interests. This will enhance and energize your life and give you new dimensions to share with your students.

24.

Remember that your students
are still learning and developing.
Be patient with growing minds
and spirits.

ART
TIME

25.

Humor can be a powerful tool.
Use it gently, wisely, and never
to hurt.

26.

Take care of yourself psychologically. Deal with your own needs and issues, so that you don't try to get your needs met by your students.

27.

Look to your fellow teachers for support, understanding, advice, and laughter. They can be sources of wisdom and strength.

28.

Feel good about yourself; give yourself a solid grounding in knowing you're OK. People feel good about you when you feel good about yourself.

29.

Realize that when you're secure, you can deal with a child's insecurity; when you're at ease, you can reassure a child's fear. Taking care of yourself helps your students.

30.

Countless times during the day, you face the choice: you can value or you can humiliate; you can affirm or you can dehumanize. Make your choice consciously.

31.

Remember how difficult it can be to be a child—how fragile and vulnerable children are in a world where they don't know all the rules, where they're unsure of themselves but don't want to show it. In this world, you can be a caring guide.

32.

When the day is difficult, when your morale is low, recall why you became a teacher. Recall the times you knew this had been the right choice.

33.

Recognize that you are the adult and your students are still children. But recognize also that you have an inner child that needs your attention and care. Don't let your needy inner child interact with your students.

34.

Know that your students
are smart in different ways.
Use different learning
techniques to reach all the
types of intelligence they have:
verbal, logical, visual, bodily,
musical, interpersonal, self.

35.

Cherish each student's uniqueness as part of the rich diversity of God's creation. Affirm all children's uniqueness, their varied talents, their different cultural backgrounds.

36.

Inspire your students. Let them know that they can make a difference, that the world can be better because of their existence.

37.

Believe in the limitless
potential of human beings.
When you expect the best from
your students, you'll get it.

38.

You have the ability to touch lives in countless, wonderful ways. Give thanks that you're a teacher!

Karen Katafiasz taught high school students for eight "illuminating and memorable" years. A writer and editor, she is the author or co-author of six other Elf-help Books and *Finding Your Way Through Grief.* She is currently director of communications for the Sisters of St. Benedict of Ferdinand, Indiana.

Illustrator for the Abbey Press Elf-help Books, **R.W. Alley** also illustrates and writes children's books. He lives in Barrington, Rhode Island, with his wife, daughter, and son.

The Story of the Abbey Press Elves

The engaging figures that populate the Abbey Press "elf-help" line of publications and products first appeared in 1987 on the pages of a small self-help book called *Be-good-to-yourself Therapy*. Shaped by the publishing staff's vision and defined in R.W. Alley's inventive illustrations, they lived out author Cherry Hartman's gentle, self-nurturing advice with charm, poignancy, and humor.

Reader response was so enthusiastic that more Elf-help Books were soon under way, a still-growing series that has inspired a line of related gift products.

The especially endearing character featured in the early books—sporting a cap with a mood-changing candle in its peak—has since been joined by a spirited female elf with flowers in her hair.

These two exuberant, sensitive, resourceful, kindhearted, lovable sprites, along with their lively elfin community, reveal what's truly important as they offer messages of joy and wonder, playfulness and co-creation, wholeness and serenity, the miracle of life and the mystery of God's love.

With wisdom and whimsy, these little creatures with long noses demonstrate the elf-help way to a rich and fulfilling life.

Elf-help Books

...adding "a little character" and a lot
of help to self-help reading!

Nature Therapy	#20080
Elf-help for Healing from Divorce	#20082
Music Therapy	#20083
Elf-help for a Happy Retirement	#20085
'Tis a Blessing to Be Irish	#20088
Getting Older, Growing Wiser	#20089
Worry Therapy	#20093
Elf-help for Raising a Teen	#20102
Elf-help for Being a Good Parent	#20103
Gratitude Therapy	#20105
Garden Therapy	#20116
Elf-help for Busy Moms	#20117
Trust-in-God Therapy	#20119
Elf-help for Overcoming Depression	#20134
New Baby Therapy	#20140
Grief Therapy for Men	#20141

Living From Your Soul	#20146
Teacher Therapy	#20145
Be-good-to-your-family Therapy	#20154
Stress Therapy	#20153
Making-sense-out-of-suffering Therapy	#20156
Get Well Therapy	#20157
Anger Therapy	#20127
Caregiver Therapy	#20164
Self-esteem Therapy	#20165
Take-charge-of-your-life Therapy	#20168
Work Therapy	#20166
Everyday-courage Therapy	#20167
Peace Therapy	#20176
Friendship Therapy	#20174
Christmas Therapy (color edition) $5.95	#20175
Grief Therapy	#20178
Happy Birthday Therapy	#20181
Forgiveness Therapy	#20184
Keep-life-simple Therapy	#20185

Celebrate-your-womanhood Therapy	#20189
Acceptance Therapy (color edition) $5.95	#20182
Acceptance Therapy	#20190
Keeping-up-your-spirits Therapy	#20195
Play Therapy	#20200
Slow-down Therapy	#20203
One-day-at-a-time Therapy	#20204
Prayer Therapy	#20206
Be-good-to-your-marriage Therapy	#20205
Be-good-to-yourself Therapy (hardcover) $10.95	#20196
Be-good-to-yourself Therapy	#20255

Book price is $4.95 unless otherwise noted.
Available at your favorite giftshop or bookstore—
or directly from One Caring Place, Abbey Press
Publications, St. Meinrad, IN 47577.
Or call 1-800-325-2511.